IF SPEECH IS SILVER, THAN SILENCE IS GOLD.......

FROM- UMANG KOCHAR

IT SHOULD NOT
MATTER TO YOU
WHAT THE OTHER
HAS DONE OR
NOT DONE FOR
YOU.

YOU MUST DO
THE RIGHT
THING BY ALL.

YOUR OPINION OF ANOTHER CANNOT BE JUST IF IT IS BASED ONLY ON YOUR PERSONAL EXPERIENCE.

DO NOT COUNT THE PEOPLE WHO HAVE WRONGED YOU COUNT THE NUMBERS YOU HAVE WRONGED.

THE VEHEMENE
WITH WHICH YOU
DENOUNC
ANOTHER,
INDICATES THE
EVIL WITH YOU.

NEVER JUSTIFY THE WRONGS YOU DO, OR ELSE, THOSE SAME WRONGS WILL VISIT YOU.

IF YOU CONDEMN OYHERS, YOU WILL BE UNABLE TO SEE THE TRUTH PERTAINING TO YOURSELF, YOU WILL FIND ONE DAY THAT YOU HAVE CEASED TO

CONDEMN OTHERS.

THE ONE, WHO
LOVES, DOES
NOT SEEK THE
FREEDOM OF
"DOING AS HE
LIKES".

HE GIVES
HIMSELF TO THE
OTHER FOR THE

WELFARE OF THE OTHER.

ANGRY WITH SOMETHING?

MENTALL PLACUPO HISHE THE CONOF E OR, D EFECT PEASTHE LORD HAS COME IN THIS FORM TO YOU! YOUR

ANGER WILL DISAPPEAR.

TO BE LOVED

IS

THE HIGEST

BLESSING TO

LOVE

IS DIVINE.

HE WHO LOVES
IS
EVER JOYOUS IN
HIS OWN LOVE.
HE DOES NOT
SEEK LOVE.
SINCE THERE ARE
NO
EXPECTATIONS,

THERE IS NO NHAPPINESS.

JUST AS A
MOTHER CAN
NEVER HARM HER
CHILD.
SO ALSO,
THOSE WHO
LOVE,
ATTEMPT TO LIFT
UP OTHERS
NEVER TO LOOK

DOWN UPON THEM.

LOVE NECESSARILY FLOWS FROM A GRATEFUL HEART.

IF YOU BELIEVE IN LOVE, YOU WILL LOVE.

IF YOU BELIVE IN MAGNANIMOUS, YOU WILL BE MAGNANIMOUS.

IF YOU BELIVE IN EMANCIPATION,

YOU WILL GIVE FREEDOM TO ALL.

NEVER SEEK JUSTICE AND DO NOT JUDGE. UNLESS YOU TOTALLY IMPARTIAL YOU CANNOT DO EITHER WITH GRACE.

A SEEKR HAS FAR MORE INTEREST IN THE UPKEEP OF HIS INTEGRITY THAN IN THE SOCIAL WORK HE IS ABLE TO PERFORM.

GODNESS IS AN UNCONDITIONAL HABIT AND UNVERSALLY APPLICABLE.

IF APPLIED ONLY TO A CHOSEN INDIVIDUAL, IT IS MERELY A BUSINESS OF

"GIVE AND TAKE".

THOSE WHO ACCEPT THE GENEROSITY OF OTHERS WITH GRATITUDE SET UP A CHAIN OF GENEROSITY, PERFORMING MANGNANIMOUS

DEEDS TO AID THEIS FELLOW BEINGS.

HUMILITY, LOVE COMPASSION, MANGANIMITY THESE ARE SOME OF THE PRECIOUS JEWELS EVERY SEEKER MUST ADORN HIMSELF WITH IN

PREPARATION TO MEET WITH HIS BELOVED LORD.

THE MAN WITH GRATITUDE WILL DEVELOP SELF RESPECT.

HE WILL NOT TOLERATE EVEN THE SMALLEST DISHONOURABLE QUALITY WITHIN HIMSELF.

HE IS HIS OWN FRIEND.

THE LIGHT
WITHIN YOU IS
THE
LUMINESCENCE
OF LORD.
WHY
SUPERIMPOSE IT
WITH THE
DARKNESS OF

DESIRE AND PETTY WANTS?

THE
MATERIALISTIC
MAN GOES TO
THE LORD WHEN
HE EXPERIENCE
FAILURE IN THE
WORLD.

THE DEVOTEE
APPROACHES THE

LORD, HAVING
GAINED
MASTERY OVER
THE
MATERIALISTIC
WORLD.

THINK WELL OF OTHERS. AIM AT GIVING THEM HAPPINESS.

THIS WILL LEND AN ATMOSPHERE OF PEACE TO YOUR MIND.

THE LEGACY ALL PARENTS SHOULD GIVE TO THEIR CHILDREN,

IS

AN INSURANCE POLICY

IN HAPPINESS; BUT THE PREMIUMS MUST BE PAID TODAY, DURING THEIR UPBRINGING.

WE ARE UNHAPPY
BECAUSE WE
SEEK HAPPINESS.
HE
WHO
ENCOURAGE ALL
SITUATIONS
WITH
EQUANIMITY,
SHALL FIND

HAPPINESS
INVEITABLY.

IF YOU WANT TO
BE TRULY HAPPY,
RELINEUISH ALL
EXECTATIONS
AND RIGHTS
OVER THE
OTHER.
LAY YOURSELF AT
THE SERVICE OF
ALL, KEEPING

DEATH AS A
WINTNESS,
AS ANE DAY YOU
SHALL
INVEVITABLE LIE
AS DUST AT THE
FEET OF ALL.

EMOTIONAL DEPENDENCY CAN NEVER GIVE YOU UNCONDITIONAL JOY.

IT IS THE GIVER WHO FIND HAPPINESS.

HAPPINESS DOES NOT INCREASE WITH THE INCREMENT OF MATERIAL POSSESSIONS, NOR UNHAPPINESS THOUGH LACK OF THEM.

DIVERT THIS
MIND FROM THE
MATERIAL
WORLD AND LET
IT FIND ITS
REFUGE AT THE
LORD'S FEET.

THAT IS THE
TRUE
PROTECTION AND

INSURANCE OF HAPPINESS.

WHY SEEK HAPPINESS OUTSIDE WHEN YOU ARE YOURSELF THE ETERNAL FOUNTAIN OF JOY?

GIVE HAPPINESS TO ALL

WHO SURROUND YOU, AND YOU WILL GAIN ABIDING PEACE.

THE AIM OF
SADHANA IS TO
REMOVE THE
EVER ENGULFING
AND ILLUSIVE
IGNORANCE THAT
MAKES YOU
BELIEVE THAT
YOU ARE OTHER
THAN THE SELF.

IT IS ONLY THIS MISCONCEPTION WHICH HAS TO BE REMOVED.

DO NOT TRY TO HURRY YOUR SADHANA BECAUSE IT IS THE EGO WHICH HURIES.

LET YOUR PACTICE BE STEADY AND

FULL OF
INTEGRITY.

SADHANA IS PRACTICE IN INDEPENDECE.

YET IT NECESSARILY CONNOTES THE SURRENDERING OF ONE'S INDEPENDENCE.

BE CONSCIOUS OF THE DIVINE

IN YOU

IT WILL NEVER FAIL YOU.

EVERY ACTION THAT TAKES ONE TOWARDS THE SELF IS MERTORIOUS.

WHATEVER TAKES US AWAY FROM THE SELF IS SINFUL.

MAKE THE BEST USE OF SHORT TIME WE HAVE HERE IN THE UNIVERSE.

LET THERE BE A CONSTAND ENQUIEY "WHO AM I?"

FEEL THE PRESENCE OF GOD ALWAYS.

MAKE THE DIVINE PRESENCE A REALITY.

THE ONE WHO
PERFROMS
SELFLESSS
ACTIONS IS
GRATEFUL TO
THE RECIPIENT
OF THE FRUITS
OF SUCH
ACTIONS,

BECAUSE THE OTHERS HAS MELTED HIS HEART AND GIVEN HIM A TASTE OF HIS OWN COMPASSION.

Faith is freedom not subordination. Faith releases you from the limitations of your own ideas, ideologies and concepts.

Faith takes one to the realms of the transcendental. The one who possess unquestioning faith is not a fanatic he is a true son of the lord.

GIVE NO
EXCUSES FOR
NOT DOING
WHAT THE LORD
SAYS.

THERE SHOULD
BE EVERY
JUSTIFICATION
FOR DOING ALL
HE HAS SAID. DO

NOT DISREGARD EVEN A SINGLE WORD.

IF YOU WEAR
THE SPECTACLES
OF
KNOWLEDGE AND
CARRY WITHIN
YOUR HEART A
STRONG
FAITH IN
LORD, YOU
WILL BE ABLE

TO BEHOLD
THE LORD
AS CLEARLY
AS YOU CAN
SEE AN
OBJECT UPON
THE PALM OF
YOUR HAND.

IF YOU WISH TO SEE THE LORD, PRESENT TO HIM YOUR BODY, MIND AND INTELLECT UNIT. HE WILL BE MANIFESTED IN YOU.

THE DAY ONELEARN TO SURRENDER ONESELF COMPLETELY IS THE DAY OF SELF REALIZATION.

IF ALL YOU DO IS SURRENDERED AT THE FEET OF THE MASTER, THEN THE CONSTANT PERFORMANCE OF HIS WILL CLEASE YOU.

SURRENDER IS TO OBEY THE ORDINANCES OF THE LORD WITH UNQUESTIONING FAITH.

SURRENDER CONNOTES A LIFE OF SERVICES TO MASTER, DOING EVERYTHING FOR HIS GLORY, AND SEEKING NOT EVEN JOY IN RETURN.

WHEN YOU HONESTLY SAY "IT IS NOT MY WILL THAT IS IMPORTANT, BUT THINE O LORD!"

THE SECRET OF SURRENDER SHALL BE

REVEALED TO YOU.

SURRENDER
GIVES ONE
ABSLOUTE
FREEDOM, AND
TAKES AWAY ALL
ONE'S
LIMITATIONS
AND WORRIES.
ONE SUDDENLY
BECOMES

EXTERMELY RICH IN THE SPIRIT OF THE LORD.

HE WHO CLAIMS THAT HE LIVES FOR THE LORD AND HAS YET NOT ATTAINED DETACHMENT, IS MISTAKEN ABUT HIS GOAL. ONE WHO LIVES FOR THE GOAL. ONE,

WHO LIVES FOR THE LORD, WILL AUTOMATICALLY RENOUNCE THE FRUITS OF HIS ACTIONS.

www.ingramcontent.com/pod-product-compliance
Lightning Source LLC
Chambersburg PA
CBHW050807290526
45792CB00001B/13